C. S Durand

Observations on leprosy and its treatment

C. S Durand

Observations on leprosy and its treatment

ISBN/EAN: 9783741151484

Manufactured in Europe, USA, Canada, Australia, Japa

Cover: Foto ©ninafisch / pixelio.de

Manufactured and distributed by brebook publishing software
(www.brebook.com)

C. S Durand

Observations on leprosy and its treatment

OBSERVATIONS

ON

Leprosy and its Treatment,

BY

C. S. DURAND, M. D.,

Harda. Central Provinces, India.

MADRAS:

PUBLISHED BY THE AUTHOR

AT THE M. E. PUBLISHING HOUSE, MOUNT ROAD.

1896.

Price One Rupee.

PREFACE.

WHEN first beginning the study and treatment of leprosy the writer was strongly impressed with the general resemblance of the disease to certain forms of ergot poisoning. Upon a more careful investigation of both, the similarity even in the most minute particulars appeared truly astonishing. It was this similarity that suggested the use of secale cornutum in the treatment of leprosy, and the results from its use during the past two years have been highly satisfactory.

This little book is not written as a *treatise* on leprosy. It has been the idea of the writer only to record some practical observations on the disease, to call attention to the similarity between it and the action of Ergot in poisonous doses, and to publish records of some of his own cases. If this remedy proves as successful in all hands as in the writer's, it will be an incalculable blessing to the worst afflicted portion of humanity as well as a great help and comfort to those who have the care of lepers. These considerations in addition to many personal inquiries from friends as to the treatment of leprosy, prompt the publication of this little volume.

Most of the symptoms of ergot poisoning given are from the "*Encyclopaedia of Materia Medica*" by Dr. T. F. Allen, to whom grateful acknowledgment is due.

CONTENTS.

LEPROSY OF ANTIQUITY.

WE have no means of certain knowledge whether this disease has or has not always appeared in the same form, with the same pathological characteristics as we see it in these days. But from the diagnostic signs given in the thirteenth chapter of Leviticus the inference is at least very strong that several diseases which we now know to be entirely distinct, were in the time of Moses classed together as leprosy. The disease now called Leucoderma, in which the skin turns white in spots, usually spreading more or less, even covering the entire body in not a few cases, is called leprosy in the chapter just mentioned. But it is worthy of remark that a distinction is made between simple leucoderma *without ulcers* and the same or other diseases with ulceration. " Then the priest shall consider : and behold, if the leprosy have covered all his flesh, he shall pronounce him clean that hath the plague. It is all turned white : he is clean. But when raw flesh appeareth in him he shall be unclean." (Lev. xiii, 13, 14.) The 13th and 14th chapters of Leviticus show how exceedingly careful the Israelites were commanded to be to completely segregate their lepers, even going so far as to err in all probability many times, on the side of safety. This inference is clear from the passage on the rites and sacrifices in cleansing the leper. The sacrificial rites were for ceremonial cleansing and not for physical healing as is distinctly implied in the

first part of Lev. xiv. The ceremonies were
to be performed *after* the leper was healed,—
after the disease had disappeared. Therefore,
from our own observation of the disease now
called leprosy, knowing that true leprosy has
no tendency to spontaneous recovery, and no
therapeutic measures are enjoined in the scrip-
ture to which we have been referring, the only
tenable position is that the cases of recovery
contemplated in the law of cleansing must
have been, not true leprosy, but leucoderma,
eczema, simple ulcer, etc., all of which had
been pronounced leprosy by the priests and the
sufferers segregated for the safety of the city
or camp.

The cases of Naaman and Gehazi, recorded
in the fifth chapter of second Kings is another
illustration of the uncertainty of the disease
or diseases called leprosy, or perhaps more
strictly, of the wide application of the term.
In pronouncing the curse upon Gehazi, Elisha

said, " ' The leprosy therefore of Naaman shall cleave unto thee, and unto thy seed forever.' And he went out from his presence a leper as white as snow." (II Kings, v, 27.) From this it is practically certain that the disease with which Naaman was afflicted was leucoderma, because, " The leprosy of Naaman shall cleave unto thee" (Gehazi), and the latter went out from the prophet's presence " a leper as white as snow." The turning white of the skin is no part of true leprosy as understood now, hence Naaman's disease must have been something else, leucoderma in all probability.

The strong presumption is, however, that leprosy as we know it to-day existed also in the time of Moses, and that the lepers were doomed, according to the law referred to, to banishment from their homes and families, sitting outside the towns, cities or camp in a condition of loneliness and wretchedness unknown in our time.

The foregoing observations are intended for the very practical and useful purpose of assisting those who have not become experts in diagnosis to distinguish between true leprosy and the disease most frequently confused with it, namely, leucoderma. It should be borne in mind that the latter is an affection of the pigment layer of the skin in consequence of which the coloring matter, which gives the individual what we call " *complexion*"—color of the skin, —becomes absorbed leaving the skin a pinkish white. It is as distinct from the disease we call leprosy now, as is rheumatism from typhoid fever. At the same time white spots do appear in some cases of true leprosy, but the writer is quite of the opinion that these are as distinct and separate a complication as bronchitis or pneumonia would be. (An apparent exception is sometimes seen in true leprosy when a finger or toe drops off leaving a white spot when the place heals. But it is only apparent, for the place of the former ulcer is white because it is covered with imperfect skin—cicatricial tissue. These pinkish white spots also often remain after the healing of ulcers from burns).

TRUE LEPROSY.

A S this little book is intended rather as a practical guide in the treatment of leprosy than as a scientific treatise on the subject, and for nonprofessional readers as well as for members of the medical profession, the pathology of the disease need not be minutely entered into. Some observations however, will be necessary in order to a clear understanding of the subject.

Writers usually recognize two forms of leprosy, the Anaesthetic and the Tubercular.

The latter form is comparatively rare. In the opinion of the writer it presents characteristics differing sufficiently from the usual form of the disease to merit a different name altogether. From this and the additional fact that the remedy mentioned in these pages corresponds only to anaesthetic leprosy, the term "leprosy" will be restricted to that disease in all the following remarks.

Leprosy is essentially a gangrene, due to impaired nutrition in the extremities. The immediate cause of the impaired nutrition is the contraction of the smaller blood vessels and consequent diminished blood supply. The term "anaesthetic" has been applied because of the loss of sensation in the diseased parts. Not only is there entire absence of pain in a fully developed case of leprosy, but so complete is the anaesthesia that the affected part may be burned, or cut without causing the slightest suffering. Indeed, according to the

writer's observation, nearly all the ulcers in
the dry form, (lepra sicca), may be traced to
burns of which the patient was unconscious.
Handling hot vessels or firebrands in cooking
and holding the hot *chillam* (pipe) in smoking
furnish ready and constant means of getting
burned, especially on the hands.

Leprosy appears in two forms, the dry and
the suppurating. These might be appropri-
ately termed respectively, Lepra sicca, and
Lepra Suppurativa. These two forms present
the common characteristic of anaesthesia but
differ in other particulars. In the dry form,
or lepra sicca, the fingers or toes lose their
sensation, the flexor tendons contract, and dry
gangrene supervenes, when joint by joint the
fingers or toes, or both, drop off without bleeding and without pain. When a joint of a
finger or toe separates, it leaves a slight ulcer
as might be supposed, but this often heals
spontaneously in a short time.

In the suppurating form of the disease, when a finger or toe drops off it is with a great deal of foul suppuration. Not only is the suppuration profuse and offensive at the joint in the process of separation, but ulcers apparently spontaneous, but possibly traumatic, appear on other parts of the body, the dorsum or soles of the feet, the palms of the hands, the arms, legs or thighs. These ulcers suppurate profusely, the discharge being remarkably offensive.

These two forms, the dry and the suppurating are manifestations of the same disease. They may in turn exist in the same individual. It seems to depend chiefly upon the constitution of the patient whether the disease assumes one form or the other. In any case, as death approaches suppuration usually appears in a very marked degree.

COURSE, DURATION, AGE AND SEX.

THREE stages in leprosy are well marked
and nearly or quite constant. Two or
all three of these may exist at the same
time but not in the same part of the body, as
finger or toe. These stages are regular in the
order of their appearance but they run almost
insensibly one into the next, so that it is difficult to say exactly when one ends and the
next begins, but when a certain stage is well
developed there is no mistaking it.

The first stage is that of Formication. The
imagination of the individual sufferer suggests

his description of the sensation which is nearly always expressed as a feeling of ants crawling in or under the skin. Sometimes the word used to describe the sensation is " tingling" or " prickling." In a few cases the sensation of burning is added to that of formication. Still more rarely noticed is a sense of coldness. These sensations are nearly always noticed first in the fingers or toes, advancing gradually up the arm or leg.

The second stage is that of Anaesthesia. It is in this stage that the two forms of the disease usually separate. In the form which seems most aptly termed *lepra sicca*, the fingers or toes as the case may be, swell slightly, turn blackish in color and look dead, as they are nearly in fact, and (in case of the fingers) become permanently flexed, usually at the middle joint. All the tissues become so rigid that it seems as if the finger would break at the joint sooner than straighten. It is in short, a perfect picture of dry gangrene. After a time the swelling disappears and a condition of atrophy supervenes which is a real death and drying up of the parts affected. (The anaesthesia established in this stage continues to the end.)

In the suppurating from, *lepra suppurativa*, swelling follows the stage of formication as in that just mentioned. But there is no drying up and atrophy. The affected parts remain swollen, soft, and dead looking, ulcerating upon the slightest provocation or even without any apparent provocation at all.

During the second stage or even toward the end of the first, the ears, nose and lips are often affected with what seems to be a true hypertrophy, as it is a permanent increase in size without any special signs of inflammation or gangrene. The nose becomes thick and unsightly, the lips thicken and the lobes of the ears increase in length sometimes nearly an inch. This hypertrophy of the three most prominent features gives to the leper that forbidding and repulsive appearance which once seen can scarcely be forgotten. Often too, the disease attacks the vocal organs when the voice becomes rough and rasping, or harsh and sibilant, while in many cases it is lost altogether. The eyes are frequently affected also but by no means always. Leprophthalmia is the term applied when the disease attacks the eyes.

The third stage is that of Disarticulation. The length of time from the appearance of the disease until this stage is reached is very variable. A whole finger or toe may drop off within a year in some cases while in others five or even ten years may elapse from the onset of the disease before a single joint is lost. The affected parts drop off at the joints, but not necessarily one joint at a time. A whole toe not infrequently drops off in a single piece, while fingers as a rule, drop one joint or at most

two joints at a time.   In many cases the nails
are the first to drop off.

As to the duration of leprosy, or the probable length of time a leprous person may live
after contracting the disease there are not sufficient data upon which to base a reliable opinion.
Leprosy is essentially chronic and usually runs
a slow but sure course.   A person contracting
the disease in early manhood or womanhood
may live for twenty or thirty years.   A few
cases have been known to live forty years.   The
average duration at certain places has been com-
puted but results differ widely, being twelve
years in one place and above eighteen in another.   Roughly stated, fifteen years as the
average would not be far wrong.

The termination of leprosy when left to nature may be regarded as invariably fatal.   The
patient does not die of the lesions described
above, but the disease goes on from bad to
worse attacking the nose, palate, pharyngeal

walls, the larynx or other organs of the body
till the sufferer becomes one mass of diseased
tissue, when some sudden complication as
bronchitis or diarrhoea closes the scene.

No age is exempt. While in the greater
number of cases the disease begins in middle
life, or earlier, about the 25th to the 30th year,
many cases begin in childhood and nearly as
many in old age. The writer has observed
cases which began as early as the fourth or
fifth year of life, and others which began after
the seventieth year.

Men are more subject to leprosy than women,
the ratio being not far from that of three to
two.

PATHOLOGICAL PECULIARITIES.

IN some cases instead of the usual turning black and withering or suppurating in the second stage, the skin remains nearly normal in appearance and a casual examination shows little trace of disease. But upon careful palpation the flesh seems of a flabby consistency which is really the case, due to the absorption of some of the subcutaneous tissues. In these cases the fingers are flexed, but they can be straightened by the application of a little force, flexing again as soon the force is removed. In these cases the tissues are not rigid as in the usual dry form of the disease, but the extensor muscles are nearly or quite paralyzed, while some of the flexor muscles, (the flexor brevis probably), are permanently contracted.

In these cases when the third stage is reached even the bones begin to absorb. This peculiarity is commoner in the hands than the feet, though the latter are sometimes affected in the same way. If it is the hands that are affected, the metacarpal bones partially absorb, sufficient to cause the hands to diminish in size and twist out of shape. The portion of muscles that may remain in the hands are completely paralyzed, so the hands are useless. If the feet are affected the same general phenomena occur. The feet become soft and flabby, the soft tissues partially absorb and part of the bones as well, so that walking becomes quite difficult or impossible.

Another most striking peculiarity is seen in the feet in a few cases. Instead of the dropping off of the toes in the third stage, the metatarsal bones entirely absorb away, leaving the toes, or such remnants of them as are not also absorbed, on a stump of a foot only about half as long as it originally was. This is one of the most astonishing phenomena in all pathological anatomy. But the fact of toes, or parts of toes with the nails still intact, clinging to the stump of the foot with the metatarsal bones gone leaves no doubt as to what has taken place.

CAUSES.

THE cause of leprosy is still undiscovered. Much labor has been expended in search of the cause and much argument to bolster up various theories from time to time, but so far as the writer is aware, no theory has been hitherto suggested that fits all the facts.

Heredity as a cause may be dismissed with the remark that as every one who has had even a *little* opportunity for observing knows, many persons, including some Europeans after a comparatively short residence in India, contract the disease with no history of heredity whatever. So, while it is true that children of leprous parents do sometimes themselves fall victims to the disease, the number is so small that the theory of mere coincidence in those cases seems at least as probable as that of heredity. A *predisposition* to leprosy may in many cases be hereditary, but not the disease itself.

The theory of contagion is not so easily disposed of. It is well known that some Europeans, as just remarked, have contracted leprosy after a short stay in India. It is difficult with our present knowledge, to account for these cases on any other theory than that of contagion. At the same time, when we consider the constant opportunities of contagion in lepers going about every where, often handling pieces of money which pass into circulation, and even selling food stuffs in the bazaars, not to mention leprous women cooking food for their untainted households as is undoubtedly done in hundreds of instances, the fact that a vastly greater number of persons do not contract leprosy leads us to look elsewhere for at least the *chief* cause. Popular belief in the theory of contagion is expressed in laws for the segregation of lepers, and where laws do not exist, in public and private efforts to enforce segregation. This popular belief has been more or less prevalent from the time of Moses until the present day.

Thus far, no theory of causation has been advanced which proves conclusive or satisfactory. Some considerations which suggest looking in quite another direction for the cause seem worthy at least of careful consideration. The chief characteristic of leprosy is gangrene, if indeed that does not constitute the whole disease. A gangrene so similar to that of leprosy that the same words may be used to describe it, often follows the use of rye as food when it is mixed with the poisonous fungus of ergot

(Secale Cornutum.) As will be seen by comparing the remarks on secale cornutum with those on leprosy the ergot poisoning runs a similar course to leprosy from beginning to end. The smut of Indian corn (maize), also in poisonous doses, produces tingling and numbness in a similar way : although less is known of the pathogenetic action of the corn smut, (Ustilago Maidis) than that of Ergot. The fact that "spurred rye" produces a gangrene so near like leprosy, and that no other kind of poison, so far as now known does so, makes it seem within the bounds of possibility that the cause of leprosy may be sought and found among the various food grains of this country.

PREVALENCE OF LEPROSY.

THERE is perhaps no other subject in reference to which statistics are so unreliable as in this. Even when the utmost care is exercised, the actual work of counting the lepers which also involves diagnosis, must in such a vast country as India, be left to persons very little skilled in differentiating diseases. In the aggregate, therefore, many cases of syphilitic and other ulceration will be classed as leprosy and counted as such. But this difficulty is trifling compared to that of *finding all the real lepers*. When it is undertaken to count the lepers, the roadside beggars and those in the various asylums are easily found. But after close observation for several years the writer is convinced that the number of cases of leprosy among the better classes of people who stay at home and would never be counted or even *found* by the statistician, fully equals if it does not actually exceed the number of known lepers. It would be therefore quite safe to double the number returned in the census reports.

TREATMENT.

THERE are few if any other diseases which present such constant characteristics as leprosy. With the exception of the few variations mentioned under " Pathological Peculiarities," individual cases differ from each other in no important particular. Even the finer subjective symptoms are practically identical in all. This being the case the problem of finding the appropriate remedy is very much simplified. In typhoid fever, for example, so contradictory has been the experience of different physicians with the same remedy or treat-

ment that many very excellent and thoughtful
practitioners have abandoned therapeutic measures altogether, relying solely upon dietetics
and nursing. This diversity of experience and
consequent diversity of opinion is entirely due
to the fact that cases of typhoid differ one from
another in many important respects. If physicians would individualize their cases, taking
into consideration the finer subjective symptoms as well as objective, selecting their reme-
dies accordingly, there would be greater uni-
formity in results and consequent unanimity
in opinion.

If leprosy presented in different cases such
a diversity of symptoms as most other diseases
do it would be fruitless to undertake a search
for a *single* curative remedy on scientific prin-
ciples, for no one remedy could be adapted to
all cases. But according to the writer's observation, any deviation of consequence from the
usual course and symptoms of the disease as

described in these pages is exceedingly rare. The problem then, so far as drug therapy is concerned is to find a remedy which corresponds as nearly as possible to all the characteristics of leprosy. A careful reading of the records published in this book will show that Secale Cornutum possesses in its pathogenesis all possible elements of similarity to leprosy. Whether this similarity renders Ergot the curative remedy, it is not necessary to argue. Whole volumes of arguments might be written which would not be worth the ink and paper consumed. It is a matter of *pratical·demonstration.*

The diet given in the cases reported has been only the simple country foods. No special attention has been given to the diet nor to hygienic surroundings, nor has there been any *massage* or other adjuvants whatever.

The amount and frequency of the dose and the best methods of administering are matters to be decided by the collective experience of a large number of observers. The writer's own practice is given under "Directions."

In some cases during the course of the treatment violent itching occurs over the whole body. As this symptom occurs in the pathogenesis of Secale Cornutum it is quite probable that the itching is due to the action of the drug. In such cases the treatment should be suspended for a time or the medicine diluted more.

SECALE CORNUTUM.

Synonyms, *Ergota, Claviceps Purpurea, et al.*
Common names, *Ergot*, Spurred Rye.
Natural order, Fungi.

ACCORDING to DeCandolle this is a fungus which finds lodgment between the awns of rye and other cereals, blighting the grain and growing up in its stead. In former years when less was known concerning the action of this parasite upon the human system, frequent cases of poisoning occurred in several of the countries of Europe. In later years greater care in eliminating the Ergot from the rye, when present, renders cases of poisoning less frequent. The cases quoted below are mostly from poisonings occasioned by eating rye bread with more or less of the grains of Ergot ground in the flour.

According to Zeimssen, Secale Cornutum in poisonous doses causes among many other striking effects, contraction of the arterioles, especially of the extremities, to such a degree that gangrene takes place in consequence of diminished blood supply.

It is interesting to read the following symptoms of Secale Cornutum in connection with the various stages of leprosy. The authority is quoted in nearly every case.

(a) FORMICATION.

" Sensation of something Creeping under the skin." (Henning.)

" Crawling and Creeping in the skin." (Wessener.)

"Formication on the arms, legs and face."
(Taube.)

"Itching all over the body so violent as to cause the patient to tear her skin." (Hill. Effects of a large dose of Ergot in a case of metrorrhagia.) "Formication, not only in the fingers but over the whole body." (Wichmann.) "Crawling sensation, as of formication, or as if the limb were stiffened by cold or were asleep, as if it had been insensible and sensation were returning with returning warmth. This is especially noticed in the fingers and toes or often over the whole body, also on the tongue which is then painful." (Dreyssig.) Other writers mentioning formication, or crawling sensation in the skin, are Flinzer, Osswald, Wagner, Oldright, Schramm and many others.

(b) LOSS OF SENSATION.

"Loss of sensation in the tips of the fingers." (Salerne, also Taube). "Numbness in the fingers." (Marcard). " Numbness of the tips of the fingers." (Henning.) " Anaesthesia of the soles of the feet." (Pratschke). " The feet feel asleep and stiff." (Schramm). " The person generally experiences not the slightest pain in the gangrenous limb whenever pricked or cut, though motion is frequently not entirely lost." (Lang).

(c) CONTRACTION, STIFFNESS.

" Contraction of the fingers." (Wagner). " The fingers were violently contracted." (Linne). " Drawing in the fingers." (Possart). " Fingers of both hands flexed tightly into the hands so that they could be opened only with great difficulty ; relief if the fingers were extended by another person, but they immediately retracted again into the hand." (Wichmann). " Contraction of the hands." (Possart). " Immobility and stiffness of the limbs." (Marcard.) " Complete stiffness of the limbs." (Ibid.)

3

(*d*) Gangrene, Ulceration, Loss of Parts.

"Gangrene of the limbs, limbs became cold, . leaden-colored and lost all sensation." (Lang). "Real gangrene of the fingers or toes." (Richter). "Cold gangrene of the limbs." (Acta Eruditor). "The fingers and toes first became discolored, then actually gangrenous; this gangrene soon became general, even penetrating to the bones, in consequence of which, frequently during the life of the sufferers the limbs fall of." (Richter). "The parts affected by gangrene spontaneously separated from the body." (Salarne). "The dead extremity separated at the joint." (Read). "Some lose their fingers or toes from cold gangrene without pain and find them in their stockings or gloves." (Acta Eruditor). "Gangrene followed by spontaneous amputation of a finger." (Hensinger). "Gangrenous death of the feet and legs as far as the knees." (Salerne). "The ends of the toes turned purple, suppurated and fell off." (Œst Med. Woch. 1847, No. 42). "NO BLOOD FOLLOWED THE SEPA-RATION OF THE LIMB BY THE GANGRENE." (Noel, in Histoire de l'Acad, des Sciene, Ann., 1710, p. 80). "Cold gangrene and death attacked the nose, fingers, hands, arms, feet, tibiae and thighs." (Perrault).

These observations might be extended to several pages, but it is unnecessary. The reader can not fail to notice the striking similarity between the symptoms recorded above and the symptoms of leprosy.

DIRECTIONS.

THE ordinary Fluid Extract of Ergot is used. It can be had at any first class pharmacy. Take of the liquid ergot one part, alcohol (rectified spirit of wine) two parts, and water three parts. Mix and keep in a well stoppered bottle. For internal use a small teaspoonful of the dilution constitutes a dose, which should be given once a day. Use the same externally by saturating a piece of cotton wool with the medicine, applying to the ulcer and keeping in place with a light roller bandage.

This dressing should not be allowed to remain on longer than two days. It is better to renew every day though if there is little or no discharge from the ulcers it does not matter much. The medicine can be poured on without removing the dressing the second day if found more convenient. But after remaining on two days the entire dressing including the bandage should be put on fresh.

It is not claimed that the directions given as to the size and frequency of the dose and strength of the dilution might not be varied to advantage. Indeed the writer has used the remedy diluted still more with apparently as good results. It is hoped that others will experiment in these particulars and publish the results.

A course of treatment should be continued for six weeks to two months, when all traces or nearly all traces of ulceration disappear. In the two years of experience with this remedy some cases have remained well to the present time, with no treatment for about twenty months past ; while others have required occasional application of the remedy for ulcers nearly always the result of burns.

PRACTICAL DIFFICULTIES.

MANY lepers have either by nature or by acquisition, a roving disposition. They will never stop long enough in one place for a course of treatment sufficient to promise much benefit. Legitimate beggars, they travel on from village to village, partly from necessity and partly in the hope of receiving more liberal alms in the next town than in the last.

But the fact that is most astounding and that would seem entirely incredible to intelligent persons ignorant of Indian native character and having had no experience with Indian lepers is, that lepers will sometimes decline to receive treatment or neglect to come where they can get it when it costs them nothing and when others are being greatly benefitted under their own observation. Not only is that often the case, but often among the higher castes, intelligent and well-to-do lepers come for treatment for a short time until their ulcers nearly heal and they show marked improvement in every way, when they discontinue the treatment, thinking themselves well even when urged to continue longer.

The point of interest in these facts is that leprosy is not feared or dreaded by the natives of India as it is by Europeans. The natives of this country do not as a rule seem to object in the slightest degree to mingling freely with lepers. A high caste Hindu may have leprous members of his family. He will eat with them, eat the food they cook, mingling any way and every way with them or other leprous members of his caste ; but if he happens to *touch* a clean healthy low caste man he is immediately defiled ! On the other hand in well conducted leper asylums the *majority* of the inmates remain permanently. These can be satisfactorily treated. The experience of the writer justifies the belief that nearly every case of leprosy in the early stages, when the constitution and general health are fair, can be promptly arrested and held in check indefinitely, while radical cures should be common. Most cases even in the more advanced stages are quickly benefitted.

CASES.

THE following cases are from the records of Lepers treated during the past two years. The treatment given is the same as that laid down under "Directions."

I.

Paltan, Kurku, æt about 70. Admitted January 20, 1894. Disease has existed for one year. Middle toe of right foot dropped off 4 months ago. All nails but one off toes of right foot. Nose swollen and blackish. Ulcer on left elbow.

January 23. Fell and rubbed skin off left arm from a surface of 5 or six square inches.

February 17. Foot has entirely healed as has also the ulcer on the arm. Much itching all over the body. Scratches the skin till it bleeds.

From this date till March 24th had several trifling ailments which were treated according to indications.

March 30. Discharged apparently well. He returned to his village and some time afterward died of diarrhoea. His death occasioned no surprise as he was feeble as well as old.

II.

February 21, 1894. Babu, Rajput, æt 30. Leprosy for 7 years. Right hand : Thumb drawn out of shape. Two joints off each of 1st and 2nd fingers. One each off ring and little fingers, 3rd and 4th fingers flexed at middle joint—stiff. Left hand : Thumb twisted similar to right. Fingers all flexed at second joints, but intact except forefinger which has lost part of first joint by absorption. Feet also affected—great toe of either foot partially absorbed. Ulcers about the joints of several toes.

April 2nd. Both feet well. Ulcers on hands where he has burned them.

June 20. Well to all appearances.

This man has not been seen since the last report, June 1894, so it is impossible to say whether the disease has become active again or not.

III.

April 19, 1894. Krishn, Brahmin, æt about 30. Has had leprosy for 5 years. Nose and lips swollen. Hands and feet both affected. Disease advanced well into the second stage. One toe much ulcerated—looks almost ready to drop off. Nails of all the

toes of the other foot ragged and appear
as if they would soon come off. Usual
treatment.

May 17. Ulcers entirely gone. The toe that
looked ready to drop off got well. The
patient remains here till the present time
(February 1, 1896), and since May 17,
1894 has had no return of leprosy. He
came here 150 miles in an ox cart, not
being permitted by the station master to
ride on the train on account of leprosy.
Has had fever, etc., at various times for
which has been treated according to indications, but has taken no ergot in any
form since May 17, 1894.

IV.

November 1st, 1895. Ram Chand, æt 35.

Leprosy for ten years. All fingers and the
thumb of left hand gone. Thumb of right
hand little affected. Two fingers of the

right hand entirely gone and only one
joint each remaining of the other two.
Skin off both wrists and forearms (apparently from a burn) from space six inches
long and two inches wide—surface entirely raw.

December 15, 1895.   Ulcers entirely healed.
General health good.   Still under observation.

V.

October 24, 1895.   Dariyao, æt 40.

Toes nearly all gone from both feet—look
as if recently dropped off as the whole surface is ulcerated, bleeding slightly when
irritated with the shoe, and suppurating.
Very weak, can scarcely walk.   Fingers
much swollen and black—some joints off.
Ulcers on skin and various parts of body.

December 20, 1895.   Feet entirely well, fingers
much better, ulcers all healed except
one on either great trochanter which

is kept irritated by lying on it. Still under observation.

NOTE.—This is the leper whose portrait forms the frontispiece.

VI.

October 28, 1895. Brij Lal, æt about 35.
Leprosy for eight years. Metatarsal bones of both feet entirely absorbed away, part of the toes adhering to the stump of the foot. Some of the toes have dropped off while others are partially absorbed. Most of the fingers affected, some have lost one joint, others more. Large ulcer on plantar surface of right foot, also several ulcers on hands.

December 1, 1895. Ulcers all disappeared.

January 5, 1896. Ulcer four inches long on side of hand from a scald with steam.

January 20, 1896. This ulcer nearly healed. Otherwise well.

REMARKS.

The majority of cases treated have been of transient beggars who only remained a short time. But in every case so far as personal recollection serves, whenever treatment was continued as long as fifteen days marked improvement has been noticed. It is freely admitted that even two years is not sufficiently long to determine whether a cure will prove permanent. But so far, all the experience with secale cornutum indicates that it is the true specific. With a wider application, used under varying circumstances by a large number of observers the truth will be established, and the remedy will stand or fall as it should do, on its own merits.

FINIS.